Saving the Ghost of the Mountain

Published in the United States by Sandpiper, an imprint of
Houghton Mifflin Harcourt Publishing Company.
Originally published in hardcover in the United States by
Houghton Mifflin Books for Children, an imprint of
Houghton Mifflin Harcourt Publishing Company, 2009.

SANDPIPER and the SANDPIPER logo are trademarks of
Houghton Mifflin Harcourt Publishing Company.

For information about permission to reproduce selections
from this book, write to trade. Permissions@hmhco. com
or to Permissions, Houghton Mifflin Harcourt Publishing
Company, 3 Park Avenue, 19th Floor, New York, New
York 10016.

www.hmhco.com

Book design by YAY! Design
The text of this book is set in Weiss.
Snow leopard line art from *Animals: A Pictorial Archive from
Nineteenth-Century Sources*, selected by Jim Harter

Maps on pages iv and v © O. Angarag. All photographs by
Nic Bishop except those on pages 11 (top) and 39, which
are © Tom McCarthy; page 11 (bottom) © Joel Bennett;
page 46 © Simon Combes; page 61 © Keegan McCarthy.

The Library of Congress has cataloged the hardcover
edition as follows:
Montgomery, Sy.
Saving the ghost of the mountain : an expedition among
snow leopards in Mongolia. / written by Sy Montgomery;
with photographs by Nic Bishop.
p. cm.—(Scientists in the Field)
1. Snow leopard—Mongolia—Juvenile literature.
I. Title.
QL737.C23B58 2009
599.75′5509517—dc22
2008036762

ISBN: 978-0-618-91645-0 hardcover
ISBN: 978-0-547-72734-9 paperback

Manufactured in China
LEO 10 9 8 7

4500698170

For Elizabeth Marshall Thomas, strong as a snow leopard, tough as Genghis Khan —S.M.
For Jalebi, who taught me about cats —N.B.

Saving the Ghost of the Mountain

An Expedition Among Snow Leopards in Mongolia

text by **Sy Montgomery**

photographs by **Nic Bishop**

sandpiper

Houghton Mifflin Harcourt
Boston New York

RUSSIA

MONGOLIA

CHINA

O. Angarag

MONGOLIA

Ulaanbaatar

Gobi-Altai

Altai Mountains

Base Camp 1

Base Camp 2

Bayantooroi

Great Gobi

O. Angarag

Upper left: snow leopard and cub; lower left: Argali sheep and ibex (sitting); lower right: Pallas' cat; upper right: golden eagle.

Chapter 1

The Ghost of the Mountain

Tom scans the remote ridges and spurs of the Altai Mountains for a snow leopard.

**B**inoculars and spotting scope in hand, the two scientists perched on a ridge along Mongolia's Altai Mountains. That spring day, their receiver antenna had just picked up a signal from across the narrow valley: *Ping. Ping. Ping.* The sound was coming from a radio transmitter.

Tom McCarthy, the blue-eyed, bearded conservation director of the Seattle-based Snow Leopard Trust, had attached the transmitter to a collar around the neck of a big male snow leopard whom he'd captured and released a year earlier.

Tom called the leopard Blue. Along with a blue collar, Tom had given the cat a yellow tag in each ear. This way, Tom would be able to recognize him—that is, if he ever saw Blue again.

It looked like he might—soon. The scientist's heart pounded with excitement. "We knew exactly where he was from the signal," Tom said, "and it was a completely barren hillside." There was nothing to block the view. It was broad daylight, around 1:00 p.m. What luck! Now was their chance to spot the animal to which Tom had dedicated his career—the most elusive cat on the planet.

People call it "the ghost of the mountain." A pale, spotted, almost cloudlike coat makes the snow leopard uncannily invisible in its rocky mountain habitat. People live their entire life among snow leopards and never see one.

Snow leopards are as tough as they are beautiful. They survive in some of the harshest, most remote, most extreme habitats in the world. They can live at altitudes too high for trees—sometimes in places with only half the oxygen people need to breathe easily. They thrive in temperatures cold enough to freeze human tears.

With a long, thick tail for balance, a snow leopard can spring at its prey from thirty feet away. It can bring down an animal three times its size. Prowling along ridges, slinking below skyline, it's as unseen, yet as powerful, as the wind.

Snow leopards are so hard to see, so difficult to find, that the people who once lived among them thought these cats were part flesh, part phantom. Even today, almost nothing is known about them. They are nearly impossible to study.

On that day on the ridge, the scientists knew Blue was right in front of them. They scanned with their scopes. They blinked. They scanned again. But they simply couldn't see him. Standing still, his spotted coat blending into the stony

FACT

Snow leopards live in the mountains of China, Bhutan, Nepal, India, Pakistan, Afghanistan, Uzbekistan, Tajikistan, Kazakhstan, Kyrgyzstan, Russia, and Mongolia.

With large, furry, nonslip paws and a thick warm coat of fur, the snow leopard is well adapted for climbing and hunting among the snowy mountains of Central Asia.

background, the snow leopard was as invisible as a ghost.

Then the pinging got faster. Blue was moving. *We're going to see him now!* Tom thought. Again the men scanned with their scopes. They still couldn't see him.

For many minutes the men searched. Though they couldn't see the cat, the changing pitch and volume of the radio telemetry told them what Blue was doing: He walked across the barren hillside. He descended to the valley floor. He crossed the little valley and turned a corner. Then the signal stopped. Blue was gone. "The whole time," said Tom, "both of us were watching through binoculars and spotting scopes. We never saw him."

"How could we not see that cat?" Tom asked his partner. "Maybe we made a mistake." Maybe Blue wasn't really on the opposite hillside. Maybe he was on the same side as the scientists, and the radio signal was bouncing off the mountain opposite them, like an echo. This sometimes happens with radio telemetry. So the men decided to descend the ridge, cross the valley, and look for tracks where it seemed the cat should have been.

"Sure enough," said Tom, "there were his tracks. And there was a great big poop in the middle of the trail! We'd been looking right at him. That tells you why you don't see a snow leopard very often."

And why they call it the ghost of the mountain.

No wonder nobody knows how many snow leopards there are. Scientists think there may be only seven thousand left in the world . . . or only half that many. Snow leopards live scattered over a vast range in Central Asia: from the stony highlands of Russia and Mongolia through the misty mountains of China and Tibet to the remote Himalayas of India, Pakistan, and Afghanistan.

Because they live in such harsh environments, snow leopards may never have been common. But today they are so rare that they are in danger of truly disappearing. They're hunted for their beautiful fur. They're killed for their bones. (Like tiger bones, they're used in Asian medicines—but don't work.) But the worst threat to this powerful cat is actually from sheep.

Sheep? That's right. Because they eat all the grass, domestic sheep and goats raised for milk, meat, and wool drive away wild sheep and goats, snow leopards' natural prey. The hungry cats have no choice: they are forced to eat livestock. Herders then try to hunt and poison the snow leopards to prevent more losses.

That's the crisis that brought Tom to study snow leopards more than fifteen years ago. He began his research here, in a

3

Mongolia: Fast Facts

Human population: 2.4 million

Size: 565,000 square miles

Major religion: Buddhism

Money: Tughrik ("TUG-rig"); 1,000 worth about $1 U.S.

Government: Once a huge empire, then conquered by China, Mongolia was under Communist control for sixty years until 1990. Today Mongolia is an independent nation whose people elect their own leaders.

Snow leopard population: unknown

The vast and barren Great Gobi stretches to the horizon, beyond some trees that fringe an isolated oasis.

Herders graze their domestic goats in snow leopard habitat, moving them from high mountain pastures in summer to sheltered valley floors in winter.

country that many Americans can't find on a map.

Mongolia, the size of Alaska, sits in the middle of Asia. Mongolia was the home of the mighty conqueror Genghis Khan, who founded the largest land empire in the world. Mongolia is the land of the Great Gobi, the world's second largest desert (only the Sahara is bigger), which yielded the world's first discoveries of dinosaur eggs.

It's a land where people live in round, felt-covered tents and tend their roving herds of sheep, goats, camels, and yaks. It's a land of stark landscapes and rich wildlife, including the ibex, a wild sheep crowned with huge, curving horns; the world's last wild Bactrian (two-humped) camels; the ancestor of the modern horse, the takhi; and the rare and endangered Gobi bear.

Few people know another fact about Mongolia: it's where as many as one-third of the world's wild snow leopards may live. And that's why Tom came here, to try to study an animal he knew he would hardly ever see. He came to try to save a ghost from extinction.

A nearly impossible mission drew Tom up that ridge that day, searching for Blue. And that same, ongoing mission now brings him back to Mongolia. Once more, he's headed for the Altai Mountains, at the edge of the Great Gobi, on a new

5

This Mongolian woman was gathering her goats for their evening milking when her photograph was taken.

Genghis Khan

Nobody knows exactly where he was born.

Nobody knows where he is buried.

Nobody knows what he looked like.

But nobody doubts that Genghis Khan—"supreme conqueror" in Mongolian—was one of the mightiest kings the world has ever known.

He united every tribe in Mongolia. Then he conquered the kingdoms of China and the lands of the Turks and Persians. He led his armies across the mountains of Afghanistan into what is now India. After Genghis Khan died in 1227, his empire continued to grow for 150 years. His empire was as large as the continent of Africa.

His army was like no other. Most armies marched together in long columns. They moved slowly. Behind them came another long line of men carrying food and camping and cooking supplies. But Genghis Khan's army rode horses, and that was one of the keys to its astonishing success.

Every Mongol grew up as an accomplished rider. This is still true today. Outside the big cities, most Mongolian kids can ride before they can walk.

A mounted soldier makes a fearsome enemy—taller, faster, and more flexible than a foot soldier. The sound of all those approaching hooves must have terrified Genghis Khan's enemies. Sometimes his soldiers tied branches to their horses' tails to whip up dust. The dust hid their movements, and made the enemy think there were more assailants than there really were.

The Mongol warrior not only rode his horse to battle; he hunted from horseback, too. This army didn't have to travel bogged down with heavy supplies. Each man carried dried cheese and strips of cured meat to eat while they rode.

The army got fresh, nutritious milk from their horses. And when there was fresh meat from the hunt, the warrior sometimes put the raw flesh under his horse's saddle. At the end of the day, the meat would be as soft and easy to chew as if it had been cooked. The soldiers didn't need smoky campfires that might give away the army's position.

You wouldn't want to be his enemy when Genghis Khan came to town. His armies left behind pyramids of human skulls. In one city, they filled nine sacks with the ears of the enemy dead.

But in Mongolia, Genghis Khan is a hero. His name adorns vodka bottles, chocolate bars, cigarettes. Mongolians admire him for his bravery, his intelligence, and his vision.

His original name was Temujin. He was born to a woman who had been kidnapped from her rightful husband. Her new husband was murdered and the family left to starve when Temujin was twelve. Yet this boy grew up to organize one of the greatest armies on Earth. His horsemen beat every enemy, even when outnumbered two to one.

Though his armies were feared, Genghis Khan never used torture. He never took hostages. He ruled well. He proclaimed religious freedom in all the territories in his realm. He opened trade between China and Europe—not only for products but for knowledge and ideas. He created a postal system. He gave Mongolia its first alphabet. He laid down its first legal code. He even wrote the first environmental laws. He protected trees, punished polluters, and outlawed hunting during animals' breeding seasons. And because he protected their prey, Genghis Khan was probably the first leader in the world to protect snow leopards.

Today we still celebrate his legacy, sometimes without knowing it. Among his many gifts to the modern world is the word "Hurray!"

Mongolian horseman.

The sturdy horses of Mongolia helped their owners conquer most of Asia.

Domestic camels take a late-afternoon rest. Owning a white camel, like the one in the front, is considered especially lucky. Sagging humps plump and rise erect when the camel puts on weight.

8

expedition that begins today.

After he last left Mongolia, nine years passed before Tom saw a snow leopard again. And on this trip, he doesn't expect to see a snow leopard either. What he hopes for is even more important. With a small team to help him, he's trying to count snow leopards—without seeing them. He's hoping to find a way to better estimate how many snow leopards live in this high, stony desert and to see if those numbers are changing.

It's the only way he can find out if the Snow Leopard Trust's efforts to protect them are working—before the snow leopard really becomes nothing but a ghost.

Chapter 2

Danger Man and Company

Squeezed between piles of baggage, Tom tries to relax on the flight to Gobi-Altai.

he signs at the airport are in Cyrillic, with triangles and backward Ns. We Americans can't read them, but Nadia, our Mongolian colleague, can. They advise passengers to put their swords in their *checked* baggage.

We're leaving the Mongolian capital of Ulaanbaatar ("OOH-lahn-BAA-tar"). It's the coldest capital in the world, where the average yearly temperature is only 29 degrees Fahrenheit. Its residents envy Siberians their "mild" winters. We're heading five hundred miles west, to the town of Gobi-Altai.

Tom has flown this route many times. Once, he remembers, the pilot strode to the cockpit carrying a frozen sheep under his arm. On other flights, some people stood in the aisles. Seated passengers—Tom included—held other people's children in their lap.

Tom loved it. He's dreamed of travels like this since he was eight years old.

Growing up in Vancouver, Washington, with two younger brothers, Tom was always climbing trees, fishing, exploring the neighborhood forests. He read *National Geographic* magazine, poring over the photos from faraway lands. "I knew I wanted to travel and I wanted to be a scientist," he says. "I knew I would make a living outside, in the wild, and I would do it overseas."

But his career got off to a rocky start when he was twelve. "The most inquisitive thing I did with wildlife," he admits, "was sting myself with a bee!"

He wanted to see how stingers work. He caught a bee and, holding it carefully, let it sting a piece of cloth. The stinger was torn from the bee's body, along with the sac of bee venom. He wondered: *If I took that stinger out of the cloth, with that little sac attached, what if I just pricked myself with it real quick? Would it hurt?*

He soon got his answer: "Yeah, it does!"

But that didn't stop him. He kept on asking questions, making observations—in other words, doing science. Soon he found himself the first person in his family to go to college.

At the University of Idaho, Tom fell in love with wildlife biology. In his sophomore year, he married his high school sweetheart. Two months after he graduated, they had their first son. Needing money for the growing family, Tom got a job as a logger. Then he worked in a sawmill.

Three years and a second son later, Tom was still working there. His childhood dreams had stalled.

But one day, he realized it was all wrong.

10

What in the heck am I doing in a sawmill? he asked himself.

"I knew the only way to get out was to go back to school," he says. Friends from college were now wildlife biologists in Alaska, so Tom moved his family there to pursue a master's degree. He decided to study the food habits of grizzly bears and spent a lot of time picking through bear poop, trying to figure out what they had eaten.

After graduating, Tom worked for the state Department of Fish and Game in Juneau, Alaska. Among other duties, he was in charge of "problem bears"—bears who came too close to humans for comfort. Sons Kyle and Keegan would often wake up in the summers to find two or three bears in barrel traps in the front yard—bears their dad had trapped during the night. He'd move them to a place far from people later that day.

One day Tom was called to a tragic scene. A poacher had killed a female bear. The poacher cut off her claws for ornaments—and left her three tiny, helpless orphans to die. Tom found them just in time. He took them home. He built a temporary den for them on the back patio and cared for them until he found them a home in an Oregon zoo.

Tom loved working with bears. But he still hoped to work in exotic lands. A few

years later, his friend, documentary maker Joel Bennett, was filming an exciting new project: Wildlife Conservation Society biologist George Schaller was beginning a study of the snow leopard in Mongolia. Tom couldn't imagine anything better.

"Here was something nobody else does," Tom says, "learning something no one has even attempted to learn, working in this remote, rugged wilderness with a fascinating culture—and all this wrapped around a cat who's absolutely gorgeous!"

Was there a place in the study for Tom? He wrote a letter to ask. To his disappointment, the reply came: "Nothing right now."

Six months later Tom found himself in Anchorage, studying caribou. One day he was sitting in his new office. His desk was piled high with books about caribou.

When he set up his first study site in Mongolia, Tom honored his time in Alaska by flying the state flag.

Tom holds the first snow leopard he radio-collared while working with George Schaller.

He sighed. So much was already known about caribou. How could he add something new?

Right then the phone rang. It was George Schaller. He was offering Tom a chance to study snow leopards in Mongolia—"That is," the famed biologist said, "if you want it."

The job meant climbing slopes above ten thousand feet with heavy gear. Freezing winters, broiling summers. No phone. No electricity. No running water. Little pay.

Tom's answer: "You bet I want it!"

That was fifteen years and a dozen countries ago. Since then Tom has outfitted snow leopards with radio collars in Mongolia and Pakistan. He's scoured snow and dust for their footprints in India and Uzbekistan. He's collected bags of leopard poop in Kyrgyzstan and China, and worked with villagers, herders, and fellow conservationists all over the globe.

These days Tom's reputation often precedes him. "You, sir," Tom's guide in Pakistan recently said to him, "are Danger Man!" And that was *before* the snow leopard they darted together woke up unexpectedly in Tom's arms.

It's easy to see how he got the nickname. But Tom is quick to point out that wild snow leopards have never hurt people. "There has never been a case of this cat committing an

attack on humans. Never!" Snow leopards aren't dangerous, but studying them is.

In the course of his work, Tom has survived a list of perils to rival Indiana Jones. Just in the twelve months before this expedition, he was hit by a car in India, fell off a cliff in Pakistan, and caught a disease in Kyrgyzstan that left him bedridden for months. He has survived everything from a

Tom has spent years on the trail of snow leopards in the steep, treacherous mountains of Asia.

From left: Nadia, Kim Berger, Bayara, and Munkho.

helicopter crash in Alaska to snapping off a tooth. (It broke from drinking hot tea after coming in from the Mongolian cold.)

Now fifty-four, Tom is a top expert on snow leopards. And as conservation director of the Snow Leopard Trust, he's not just studying them—he is trying to save them. He knows he can't do it alone.

Let's meet the team Tom has assembled to help him on this expedition.

"**Nadia,**" twenty-seven. Her real name is Tserennadmid, but we can't pronounce it. Like most Mongolians, she doesn't use a last name. Nadia grew up in the Gobi, where her dad was studying wild camels and the Gobi bear, and helping Tom with his snow leopard study. Nadia has known Tom since she was in sixth grade—she is the same age as Tom's younger son—and

she now works for Tom as a staff biologist with the Snow Leopard Trust.

Kim Berger, forty. As a conservation biologist working for the New York–based Wildlife Conservation Society, Kim has studied pronghorn antelope in the American West, moose and caribou in Alaska, and wolves and coyotes in Grand Teton National Park. She specializes in counting animals—especially when they are too many to count one by one or so rare you never see them. This is her third trip to Mongolia. She has joined Tom to help him figure out a more accurate way to estimate how many snow leopards are left.

Bayara, thirty-eight. Trained as a teacher, like both her parents, Bayara never imagined a career protecting snow leopards. But thanks to her translation

skills, she's now Mongolian program coordinator for the Snow Leopard Trust. She helped Tom start Snow Leopard Enterprises here. She'll join us later in the expedition. Together we'll visit families who earn money by making traditional handicrafts while protecting snow leopards at the same time. Bayara loves snow leopards even though she's never seen one, except at a zoo. "That's dedication for you," Tom says, "to work for eight years to conserve an animal you've never seen."

Rounding out the team are our driver, **Munkho,** our cook, **Enkhe,** and Nic Bishop and me. Nic has come to take the photos in this book. I'm along to write the words.

Once we land in Gobi-Altai, together we'll begin one of the greatest adventures of our lives.

The Takhi's Return from Extinction

When explorer Nicolai Przewalski ("prizz-WALL-skee") brought the skull and skin of a Mongolian wild horse home to Russia in 1881, scientists proclaimed he'd found a new species. They named it Przewalski's Horse.

Of course, Mongolians knew about it all along. They called this stocky yellow horse with the short, zebralike mane the takhi ("TOK-ee").

But just eighty years after its scientific "discovery," the takhi was extinct in the wild. The last wild takhi was seen in the 1960s in the southern Gobi.

What happened? Nobody can blame the snow leopard. Though they both live in the Gobi, the leopard sticks to mountains; the takhi prefers plains.

Some people say herders' livestock may have driven the takhi away from waterholes. Most agree that Western "collectors," seeking to kidnap foals of this "new" species to display in foreign zoos, killed many takhi parents and scattered tight-knit herds.

But in the end, zoos saved the takhi. All of the twelve hundred takhi alive today are descendants of twelve caught for zoos in the wild around 1900. Dozens of zoos have bred takhi since then. By 1992 there were enough to bring back to the Gobi to establish wild herds in their homeland once again.

Today there are about three hundred takhi in Mongolia. About one hundred of them live in the Gobi. Another two hundred live in Khustai National Park, near Ulaanbaatar, where Nic took these photos.

A wild takhi mare nuzzles her foal.

Chapter 3

Journey to the Great Gobi

Expedition supplies are piled onto the van at the airport.

Munkho meets our flight in the trust's brand-new twelve-seat Russian-made Furgon—a van with a jeeplike chassis and two big gas tanks. We'll need them on a journey where gas stations are rare.

Nadia and her grandmother.

The van is overloaded before we even get in. Back in Ulaanbaatar, Munkho packed it with just about everything we'll need. Every cranny, as well as the luggage rack on top, is crammed. Tinned meat, fish and vegetables, flour, salt, sugar, tea and coffee, potatoes, carrots, and cabbages vie for space with our portable gas stove, canisters of propane, plates, pots, tents, camp furniture, first-aid kit, water filter, and scientific gear such as test tubes and data sheets. The luggage we brought on the plane—sleeping bags, hats, sunscreen, pens, books, clothes, and Nic's photographic gear—must fit into any gaps we can find.

We'll drive for thirteen hours. Curling down the map in an S-shape, we'll skirt the base of the mountains through a valley, then snake south over the Altais through a pass. Our first night's stop will be Great Gobi National Park Headquarters. The next day, Nadia's dad—the park director—can tell us where we should set up base camp for our study.

We're eager to start. But within minutes of boarding the van, we face our first delay: Nadia's seventy-five-year-old grandmother lives within blocks of the airport. It would be rude not to stop in.

Like most Mongolians who live outside big cities, Nadia's grandmother lives in a ger ("gair")—a remarkable one-room house made of wood and wool. A round, canvas-covered felt tent, the ger can be taken apart in just a few hours. It's easily moved from place to place, on camels, horses, yaks, or cars. It's perfect for herders who move their livestock to new pasture two, three, or four times a year, as half of all Mongolians do. Most wouldn't want any other kind of house.

Inside, we're treated to traditional Mongolian hospitality. As we sit cross-legged on the rug, Nadia's grandma hands us bowls of steaming "milk tea." It's more like milk soup: salty, not sweet, it smells faintly of mutton grease. Next comes a platter piled high with fried dough. Now slices of white bread with butter. Finally we're offered noodles with mutton, which she dumps with chopsticks right into our bowls of tea.

She cooked all this food on the big black stove in the center of the ger. It looks like a wood stove, but in the treeless Gobi, no one burns wood. How do they heat their homes and cook their food? Hint: it's free, abundant, lights easily . . . and comes out of the back end of an animal! Dried by the desert sun, the manure of the herders' animals makes great fuel. And it's not smelly. Honest.

As we sip our milk tea, we admire the ger. The bright orange poles holding the ceiling up are decorated with beautiful designs. They match those on the furniture—beds, chest, and the Buddhist altar—that line the curving walls. The room is cheerful, adorned with posters and family photos.

18

Ger doors are decorated with rich colors. Orange is a favorite with Mongolians.

Tom takes the delay in stride. He enjoys visiting Nadia's family. Nadia's grandmother looks pretty in her blue satin del ("dell"), the traditional quilted Mongolian robe tied at the waist with a thick sash. The conversation (which Nadia translates for us) follows a tradition, too:

"So how is the weather?" Tom asks.

"A dry summer, no rain at all."

"And was last winter mild or snowy?"

"Mild," answers the grandmother. "No zud."

"Zud" is a word for disaster, which occurs when livestock cannot find grass. There are four kinds: Gan zud, when pasture is ice-covered; Khar zud, when there is no snow at all and the grass is destroyed by the fierce, windy cold; Tsgaan zud, too much snow; and Tuuvain zud, when pasture is trampled by overgrazing.

Nadia's grandmother lives outside an airport, not in a pasture. But even so, the first, most important topic of conversation is the welfare of livestock.

And that's true for most Mongolians outside the big cities. Their sheep, goats, yaks, horses, and camels are meat, milk, and money. Their animals provide transportation, fuel, and food. Even the walls of their homes come from their animals: the felt is made from pressed camel wool.

Mongolians have lived this way for thousands of years. Fewer people live in this

Yaks are favored by herders who live high in the cool mountains. Out on the hot plains, people often milk camels instead.

nation than in the city of Chicago, yet they are spread over an area the size of Alaska, making Mongolia the world's most sparsely populated country. Even today there are as many horses here as humans, ten times more sheep than people, and even more goats, camels, and yaks.

As livestock crowds out the snow leopard's natural prey, Tom knows the cat can't survive without herders' help. "We can study the snow leopards," says Tom, "but the local people are the only ones who can save them."

We bid Nadia's grandmother goodbye and pile back into the van. The ride is hot and bumpy. Though it has 565,000 square miles within its borders, Mongolia has only 750 miles of paved road. None of it is beneath our wheels. We jounce along, sometimes bumping our heads against the roof. Tom used to drive this route two to three times a year for six years. Once, his car bounced so hard that the dashboard came loose and the wires beneath it caught fire!

Except for tire tracks, the "road" is no different from the landscape around us: an endless sea of rocks. Some are as small as gravel, others as big as camels. The Chinese call the Gobi "the dry sea." It seems to stretch forever. The Gobi covers a third of Mongolia. You can travel for days, even weeks, without seeing a tree or a car or a person.

The word Gobi means "desert" in Mongolian. But only 3 percent of the Gobi is sand. The rest is a different kind of desert: stony plains; rocky, treeless mountains; and stark scrub. It's a huge, harsh landscape. Nights are cold even in summer. Blinding dust and sandstorms can strike at any time. Mongolia is a land-locked country; no ocean breezes moderate its temperatures. Though August temperatures can reach 115 degrees Fahrenheit, snow can fall as early as September.

This land seems as lifeless as the moon. Stones. Sky. Wind. Dust. The scenery before us seems heavy with emptiness. As daylight turns to dusk, and dusk fades to night, we can't help but wonder: Can anything really live here?

Desert Dinos

The sandy southern part of the Gobi has been a lush hunting ground— for scientists who dig dinosaurs, that is.

Between 1922 and 1930, the American adventurer Roy Chapman Andrews discovered more than one hundred dinosaurs there, including the world's first dinosaur eggs. Before he found them, no one even knew how dinosaur babies came into the world. Nobody knew dinos laid eggs like birds do!

Following in Andrews's footsteps, other scientists have made more astonishing Gobi finds. One of them is a famous fossil that's like a snapshot of a dramatic dino battle that took place 80 million years ago. The two dog-size dinos, a velociraptor (like the

There were no winners in this battle. The velociraptor is lying on the left and has its hand clamped in the beaklike jaws of the protoceratops at right.

star of Jurassic Park) and a protoceratops ("pro-toe-SARE-uh-tops"), are locked in combat. The 'raptor's right-hand claws are hooked in the belly of the protoceratops, while the protoceratops chomps down on the velociraptor's other hand.

How was this moment frozen in time? Scientists think a sand dune must have collapsed on the dinos at the height of their duel. Their bones turned to fossils, entombed in the sand that killed them, until they were uncovered by a Polish-Mongolian team in 1971. You can see the fossil at the National Museum of Natural History in Ulaanbaatar.

Some of the world's roughest "roads" crisscross Mongolia. Travel in the Gobi is hot, dusty, and very slow.

Chapter 4

Remembering Red

Though our expedition takes place in August, Tom is thinking of February. When we're sweltering in 95-degree heat, Tom is remembering 40 degrees below zero. Now that he is back in Mongolia, he can't help but remember the first day he began his snow leopard study, thirteen years before.

It was a very lucky day.

Struggling to hike with heavy gear through snow deeper than his knees, he set out eight soft leghold snares, and then walked more than three miles back to his campsite. He collapsed in his ger that night. He was too tired to make anything for dinner other than canned horse meat and a block of Ramen noodles.

In the morning, back he went, up the mountain, to check his traps. The traps are designed with the cat's safety in mind. Attracted by tasty bait, when the leopard steps on the trap's trigger, a spring throws a loop made of cable up the leg and then tightens. A stop at the end of the cable prevents the loop from getting too tight. The cable is thick and soft so it won't cut the leopard's skin. So the cat can't run away, each trap is tied to a drag. (Tom used the broken steel radiators from apartments, each weighing about seventy pounds, which he had to lug up the mountain along with his other gear.) Another spring between the trap and the drag flexes when the cat pulls on it. That way the cat can't pull so fast or hard that it injures itself.

Tom didn't expect to find anything in his traps that first day. When he worked with George Schaller, they trapped for a month before they captured a snow leopard.

So Tom was not surprised to find the first

trap empty. But as he approached the second trap, he couldn't believe his eyes. There was a cat in it. But it was not a leopard. It was a lynx!

"I didn't even expect to see Eurasian lynx in the area," he said. Carefully he sedated the animal, and took its weight and other measurements. Then he turned it loose. On he went to the third snare. Nothing. And the fourth: the same. But what he found in the fifth still amazes him, thirteen years later: "It was a big old male snow leopard! Two cats in one day!"

Tom estimated the cat's weight: ninety-five pounds. He measured the amount of sleeping drug he'd need to sedate him. Carefully he filled a syringe attached to a hypodermic needle. After mounting the needle on a six-foot pole, Tom jabbed the cat with the shot in the rump. Within seconds, the leopard lost consciousness.

Working quickly, Tom detached the snare. He took out his checklist: measure the weight, length, other body dimensions. He noted them on a worksheet. With tweezers, he pulled out a tuft of fur and put it in a stoppered vial. Later, genetic tests could tell him whether this leopard was related to others he might catch. With a device that looks like a hole puncher, he put red plastic tags in both the leopard's ears. Now the leopard had a name: Red. Tom gave Red a

shot of antibiotic, to protect against infection, and he attached the radio collar.

The short hour he had so close to Red was nearly up. But then Tom gave himself a special treat, just for the pleasure of it: he stroked Red's fur. "Soft. Gorgeous. Very luxurious," he remembers.

But there wasn't much time for luxury. The drug was wearing off. Tom backed away and let the leopard recover.

Tom watched from a distance through binoculars. The cat wandered up the hillside to an overhanging rock at the base of a cliff a few hundred feet above the trail. And there Tom left him.

He picked up Red's radio signal a few days later. He followed the sound, then lost it, then found it, then lost it again. Eventually the battery died. All of Tom's snow leopards had degradable "spacers" in their collars, designed to decay over time so the cat wouldn't be stuck with a collar forever. After the battery died, Red's collar must have fallen off.

"I tracked that cat for almost four years," Tom says. "But I never saw him again."

23

Chapter 5

Bayantooroi and Beyond

A herder drives his goats through the poplars at sunset.

e wake in an oasis. Bayantooroi—site of Great Gobi National Park headquarters—means "rich in poplars." We drink in the sight of beautiful trees a hundred years old. They may be the only trees we'll see for the next four weeks.

Nadia knows these trees well—as well as she knows Bayantooroi's marshes and birds. It was here she fell in love with wildlife. But it wasn't the bears or the camels her dad was studying that first caught her attention. The path that led to snow leopards began with a little critter the size of a baseball who came home in her younger brother's pocket.

At first he didn't look like an animal at all. His head was invisible, rolled up in a protective ball covered with spines. But when he relaxed, the creature revealed bright black eyes and elflike ears. He was a long-eared desert hedgehog, found in deserts from Egypt to China.

Nadia instantly adored him. She loved watching him trundle around. She fed him meat and cookies. (In the wild, hedgehogs hunt at night for beetles and grubs.) When she wasn't playing with him, the hedgehog lived in a big box. "But he was always getting out!" Nadia remembers. "He liked to go to the kitchen." Nadia's mom wasn't happy about that. But she let the hedgehog stay.

After four or five months, the hedgehog escaped for good. But he had turned Nadia into a nature lover. With her friends, Nadia began to explore Bayantooroi's marshes. She loved going with her dad on expeditions, trying to spot Gobi bears and wild camels. When she was in sixth grade, she met Tom and his sons. They often visited with Nadia and her dad at park headquarters. Nadia and her dad visited them in their mountainous study area, a few hours' drive away. "Tom is like a second daddy to me," Nadia explained. And with *two* dads as wildlife biologists, it's no surprise she ended up being one, too!

Nadia's dad is named Mijiddorj. Tom just calls him Miji. We meet in his office to discuss our expedition. We need his advice.

Tom outlines our plan. "One of the things we're trying to improve," he tells Miji as Nadia translates, "is population monitoring. Kim, from the Wildlife Conservation Society, will help us with new statistical methods. And with Nadia, we'll be doing lots of sign surveys." We'll

The long-eared desert hedgehog emerges to hunt insects at night when it is cooler.

FACT

A deep chest with big lungs, long hind limbs for leaping, and a long, flexible tail for balance adapt the snow leopard to mountain life.

be collecting any signs we find of leopards, he explains; and finally, we'll set up a pair of cameras to try to snap a leopard's picture.

"So who could serve as a guide to take us to the best snow leopard areas?" Tom asks his friend. And there's another problem as well. We need to go where we might find signs of leopards, but we have to live there, too. "We know we have to go to habitat that's steep and rocky to find signs of snow leopards, but is there any water there?" asks Tom.

Miji is glad to help. He knows a young herder who can serve as our guide. Miji also recommends a good place for a base camp. And he offers to lead us there personally, this very afternoon.

As Miji leads the way in his jeep, we leave Bayantooroi's tall poplars behind. Ahead, a brown, barren landscape. More rocks. More dust. More jagged mountains.

Finally, two hours later, we stop in a valley 6,638 feet above sea level. We're surrounded

by steep, scree-covered slopes that tower 4,000 feet above us. A cool breeze blows. Camels lounge in the distance. A shallow stream flows nearby. With our camp filter, we'll have plenty of drinking water. We can't bathe or shower, but we can wash our faces and hands.

There is a vacant stone corral about two hundred yards away. One of the outside walls offers enough privacy to dig a hole in the dirt for a latrine.

We're home! Or we will be once we set up our tents and our very own ger. Munkho sleeps in the car; Nic and Kim and I sleep in our small private tents. But Nadia, Tom, and Enkhe choose to sleep in the ger. This snug, round house is the perfect spot to cook our meals, to store our gear, and to gather for breakfast, dinner, and discussion.

Tomorrow we will begin our search for signs of leopards—tracks, poop, and places the leopard has marked with urine

Beyond these poplars at Bayantooroi lies our destination: the Altai Mountains, where we will study snow leopards.

Our camp (at left) is dwarfed by the surrounding mountains. If you look carefully you will see camels grazing in the valley.

and scratches to warn rival leopards away and attract possible mates in the winter breeding season. Like the leopards themselves, these signs aren't easy to find.

"Not only are snow leopards rare," Tom explains, "but they only use specific areas to mark where they've been,

mostly in areas with steep, cliffy, broken slopes. Places ibex favor." These elegant wild goats are snow leopards' favorite food. "Ibex like these difficult areas, because most predators can't follow them there. Except," says Tom, "for our buddy." He puts down his binoculars to think.

"We need to find a steep habitat edge," he says. "A gently rounded or flat surface has nothing to attract a snow leopard to mark. So we need to get up high and make a plan," he announces. "Tomorrow we can reconnoiter, take a peek."

How to Erect a Ger

1. Select a spot for the door and its frame, facing south to catch the warm sun.

2. Leaving a gap for the door, unfold the five-foot-high collapsible lattice-like walls, called khana. Tie the sections together with rope.

3. Tie door frame and door to the walls.

4. In the center of the circle formed by the khana, set up the two pillars called bagana. Place the small circular ceiling piece, or tonoo, on the top between them. The hole allows smoke to escape from the cooking fire. Secure them with rope.

5. Erect the rest of the ceiling. It's formed by dozens of slender poles called uni that radiate from the tonoo like the spokes of a wheel.

6. Wrap walls and ceiling with camel felt, and cover with canvas. Secure with three ropes around the whole structure. You're home—till the next move!

29

Chapter 6
Desert Surprises

It is not uncommon for the map to be pulled out for a discussion about where, exactly, we are.

om studies the map and smiles. "This looks good," he says. It's a topographic map: lines within lines show how high and how steep each mountain is. Tom likes the places where lots of lines come close together.

"We could climb up about two kilometers and pop over this offshoot," he says, pointing to the steepest, highest spot. (Scientists often measure distance according to the metric system. One kilometer equals about 62/100ths of a mile. Multiply by .62 to convert kilometers to miles.) "I want to get up high today and get the lay of the land."

At 8:10 a.m. we set off to hike up the rocky slope.

At first it seems a brown, stony sea of rocks and dust. But then we look more closely. Among the rocks, we find the curving horn of an ibex. We see the stark skull, backbone, and shoulder blade of a camel. We're shocked to discover wildflowers growing in crevices between rocks: delicate purple asters, bright yellow flowers like daisies.

The "empty" desert begins to fill our senses. Sudden jolts of color take us by surprise. Even some of the rocks are bright with lichens. Some are electric yellow, others as orange as the painted poles of our ger. We begin to notice the scents of mint, rosemary, wild onion. Everything is richer than we expected.

We're looking for the sorts of rock faces where a leopard might have left a mark—a message intended for other leopards. But another surprise is around the bend: a message of a completely different kind, from another time. We're face-to-face with ancient pictures that people carved on these rocks, perhaps thousands of years ago.

Here an artist carved an ibex. There, a wild argali sheep. More art shows a sort of lizard-shaped animal—maybe it was a snow leopard. These carvings are known as petroglyphs ("PET-row-gliffs"). *Petros* means "rock" in Greek; *glyph* means "carving." Later in our trip, we'll find more petroglyphs—of wolves, camels, people, and beyond a doubt, a beautiful and realistic snow leopard. No one is certain why these ancient artists created these carvings. One thing's for sure, though: Mongolians have been thinking about snow leopards for a very long time.

But where are the live leopards today?

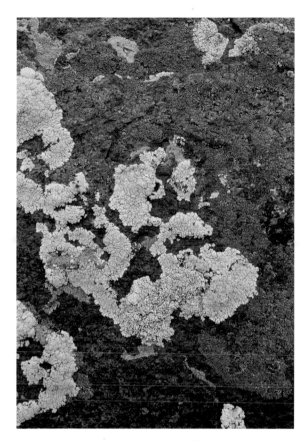

Lichens bring colors to an often barren landscape.

This ancient petroglyph shows ibex with long, curved horns being chased by wolves. Both species are rare now in Central Asia.

Tom inspects another petroglyph. From its markings this probably shows a snow leopard.

Have they left any messages for us? We continue the search.

We walk on, and discover more treasures: The den of a pika, a short-eared relative of the rabbit. The droppings of a baby camel. A two-foot-long black feather from a vulture.

We pass a number of flat rock faces. "Good areas for snow leopard sign," says Nadia, "but there is nothing. Maybe washed away by the rain."

Rain? Yes, that was another surprise. Last night it rained off and on for hours. (And those of us who didn't sleep in the ger worried our tents might blow away, with us inside!)

Up we climb. We come to another rock face. Tom looks at the bare ground carefully. "If a snow leopard marked here," he says, pointing, "its back feet would parallel the rock face as it drew its feet back here." The area of disturbed soil is called a scrape. "Then it would turn and face the other direction and spray," Tom says. Snow leopards, like many animals, leave their messages in scent.

Tom sniffs the rock face. He smells nothing. "This scrape, if it is one, hasn't been used in a long time." Disappointed, we hike on.

Then, at 10:16 a.m., Tom brightens. "Now we're talking!" he says. He's discovered what he's looking for—what we've all flown halfway across the globe to find. It's five inches long, full of hair and little red seeds.

It's a piece of poop. Tom is thrilled.

Suddenly, being a snow leopard researcher doesn't seem so glamorous anymore. Tom has come to Mongolia to sniff for pee and search for poop.

"I think my whole biological career is based on poop," he admits. "As a grad student I studied bear poop. I surveyed deer and I counted deer poop. Then I found myself looking all day for snow leopard poop, and cooking my dinner with camel poop. Poop pervades my life!"

It's no wonder. If you want to study animals, you've got to become a professor of poop. Once you do, when you find an animal's droppings, you'll be able to look into a time capsule, read a message, even count animals you can't see. No wonder dogs seem so interested in this stuff. They're on to something!

If you have pets, you probably already know some of the science of "scat" (as biologists call animal droppings). Different animals leave specific droppings: a dog's droppings look different from a guinea pig's. Sheep leave little balls; cows drop flat mud pies; meat eaters leave cigar-shaped pieces, often with pointed ends. From the scat, you can tell who was here—and from the condition of the scat, about how long ago. You can tell what the animal ate. Often you find bones, hair, or berries in scat. And from the amount of scat you find in a particular area, you can even start to figure out if that

The Professor of Poop collects a sample of snow leopard scat.

animal is common or rare. Counting scats is an important way in which scientists estimate how many snow leopards live in an area. But first scientists have to estimate how many poops an individual leopard leaves over time, and how likely a scientist is to find them.

As if he's savoring some special cheese or fine wine, Tom picks up the poop and sniffs it. Though the desert air has dried it out, "it smells pretty fresh," he says. He puts it down and breaks it in half with a stick. Whoever

33

left this scat had eaten something with hair—probably ibex, Tom thinks. "Might be snow leopard scat," he says. "Might be wolf. We'll see."

How to tell wolf scat from leopard? Many naturalists think they can tell at a glance. Tom certainly thought he knew snow leopard scat. But scientists are always testing their own hypotheses, and one day,

Tom thought he should test to see if what he thought was snow leopard scat really was. He took the scats to a laboratory, and found out about a third of the scats he thought had been left by snow leopards were really left by foxes!

How can labs tell the difference? On its way through the lower part of the digestive system, a scat picks up some of

that animal's own cells. Each cell in every body contains the sequences of genetic coding called DNA that are unique to that species and that tell how to make one animal into a snow leopard and another into a squid. Laboratory tests can look for the genetic sequences unique to snow leopards. A different set of tests can even tell individual snow leopards

apart—another way of counting members of a population.

That's why Tom and our team have come halfway around the world in search of scat. To find it, take it home, and see whose it really is. Unless we know for sure, all the estimates of how many snow leopards there are in the world might be wrong—and we'd never know.

Kim takes a reading on her global positioning unit. The hand-held device sends a signal to an orbiting satellite, which calculates exactly where and how high we are. She needs this information to fill in the data form: everything must be recorded to understand where the leopards were and when.

AREA: Gobi Altai
COORDINATES: N 45.14 132 (a little over halfway between the equator and the North Pole) and E 097 12.821 (in the eastern half of the world)
RELATIVE AGE: fresh
COLLECTED BY: TMc & N
ALTITUDE: 2,117.75 meters (Want to convert to feet? Multiply by 3.28.)

Wearing a rubber glove so her own DNA doesn't contaminate the sample, Nadia picks up the scat. She stuffs a piece of it into a vial of alcohol and stoppers it. This sample will go to a lab back in the States. Another sample is stored, with all the info, in a plastic bag.

This one is going to a different lab, where the technicians don't all wear white coats. Some wear fur coats—their own. It's a lab staffed in part by dogs.

Laboratory analysis of animal scat is very expensive, Tom explains. And depending on how busy the lab is, it can take months to get the results. But dogs can surely tell snow leopard from wolf scat in a single sniff. For a dog, telling the difference is probably as easy as distinguishing between Swiss cheese and cheddar is for you. At Working Dogs for Conservation Foundation, folks are training dogs to do just that—and tell us what they know—just like police dogs sniff out illegal

Each scat sample is carefully stored in a labeled vial filled with alcohol.

FACT

Snow leopards spend about a third of their time moving and two-thirds resting.

drugs. Captive snow leopards in zoos provide the scat so the dogs learn the "target" the trainer is looking for. They then can alert the trainer that they've found the target by barking or sitting by it. Without ever leaving their Montana homes, American dogs could help Tom count unseen leopards in Mongolia.

By 10:30 a.m. the jagged cliffs have turned to rolling hills. Tom is disappointed. Easy walking for us; no good for snow leopards. "Let's go around the corner," says Tom, "and make a decision what to do then."

We follow a narrow path worn by

the hooves of sheep, goats, and other animals. Kim takes another reading on her GPS: we're at an altitude of 7,441 feet. "Let's go up the side of this valley," Tom suggests, "and see if it's productive."

At 12:30 p.m. Kim finds an old, white cigar-shaped scat full of bones. "My guess is it's wolf," says Tom. "But it could be snow leopard. Let's take it and see."

And so it goes. A place that should be a scrape ("It would be hard for a snow leopard to resist!" says Tom) with no evidence of a leopard. Another scrape that's at least six months old.

"Should we do the next ridge?" Tom wonders aloud at 1:10 p.m. "This valley isn't doing us much good. Let's go on top and take a look." Three-quarters of the way up the slope we find a scat with the entire, intact foot bones of a marmot, a cousin of our American woodchuck. But did a snow leopard kill and eat it—or a wolf? Or a fox? Out come the bags and vials, and we trek on.

At the top of the ridge, 8,389 feet, Tom sees trails left by ibex, the leopard's favorite prey. The view is stunning, but bleak.

"Is this what you thought snow leopard

habitat would look like?" Tom asks Nic and me. "What's funny is, I go to habitats far more lush, where there are far fewer snow leopards than here in the Gobi. This area has one of the highest snow leopard concentrations anywhere."

But where are they? Where are their scats and scrapes? We follow the ridge line, placing our boots carefully on the slopes slippery with rocky scree, steadying ourselves with our walking sticks. At 3:15 p.m. we find another possible scrape. There's a big scat sitting right in the middle of it, white with age. Using a rock like a scalpel, Tom teases a tiny bone from the scat. But is it snow leopard scat? Tom sighs. "Another definitive 'I dunno.'"

By 4:00 p.m. we head back to camp—a scary scramble down a slope of frost-shattered rock. And it's even more slippery because it's raining now.

Again the unexpected. And despite so many glimpses at its wonders, so much still lies hidden in this sandless, stony desert.

The first dark drops of rain on the brown rocks tease us. They remind us of the spots on the snow leopard—the unseen animal who rules this endlessly surprising land.

A snow leopard scrape can be very hard to discern, even by Tom's experienced eye.

The rocky back of the Altai Mountains stretches more than one thousand miles from one end to the other.

Chapter 7

Remembering Green

**W**ith snow leopards, you never know what might happen next. Perhaps nobody taught Tom that lesson better than the leopard he called Green. Tom told us about her as we sat in the warm ger that night after dinner.

After catching Red and Blue, Tom had tried to track them for about a year and a half. It was extremely difficult. He seldom heard their signals. And even when he could, he couldn't keep up for long. On average, snow leopards travel six miles a day. But while they sometimes stay for days in the same valley, they can move fast. A leopard can cover hundreds of miles in a week.

Tom decided he needed a different kind of radio collar. Red and Blue had ordinary radio collars. They send signals only to the researcher's receiver. But recently, somewhat heavier, more high-tech collars had been invented. They send signals both to the researcher on the ground and to a satellite orbiting high above the earth. A computer in the satellite tracks the cat even when the scientist can't hear the signal. It records the cat's position twice every day.

Tom went back to the States and got two satellite radio collars. He hoped to put one on a male and one on a female. And when he returned to Mongolia, he brought two good assistants to help him do it: sons Keegan and Kyle, then teenagers.

That was back in January 1996. In the brutal cold and deep snow, they set up a line of twelve new traps stretching perhaps three miles along the valley where they camped. They checked them each morning.

One day in February, they discovered that one of the traps was missing, along with the seventy-pound steel radiator used to weight it down. "We knew we had something in the snare," Tom said. "But we didn't know what."

The three looked everywhere. It couldn't have just vanished! They combed the area six times. Finally they saw it: Right in the middle of the valley, beside a rock—again, almost completely invisible—was a snow leopard. One leg was hooked in the snare attached to the heavy weight.

FACT

A snow leopard can cover twenty-five miles of open desert in one night.

"She had dragged that weight less than thirty feet away from where we set it," Tom remembers. "She hadn't gone far. But there she was, and we must have walked within two feet of her three or four times . . . and never saw her."

She was small, perhaps only eighty-five pounds—and very old. Pampered in a zoo, a very lucky snow leopard might live to twenty or twenty-one. But in the wild, few snow leopards live to age ten. Life isn't easy when you must kill every meal with your mouth. Looking at Green's teeth, Tom thought she might be twelve or thirteen. And the years had not been easy.

She had three broken canine teeth. She was missing one ear. Her head was covered with healed wounds—battle scars from other leopards, perhaps. Her lip was split almost to the gum. All were old wounds. None were bleeding. She didn't seem in pain. But Tom felt sorry for her. He wondered, *Do we really want to put this big satellite collar on this old cat?*

Tom considered it carefully. "I realized, we don't catch enough cats to turn this opportunity down. So I put this rather large radio collar on her, hoping she'd be OK." They put her green ear tag in, and once she woke up from the tranquilizer, watched her go.

The collar's transmitter began immediately to send signals to the satellite. But this was in the days before e-mail. Back then the satellite system sent the info to scientists by regular mail. Fortunately, though, Tom and his sons could also follow Green on their receiver. They tracked her to another valley. The next day they heard the signal coming from the same place. The day after that, she was still there.

They worried. Was something wrong? Had the collar fallen off? Was the big collar too much for the old female? Was Green dead? They had to find out.

"I told the kids, 'You sit up on this ridge line and watch, while I go down. I think that collar's right at the base of this cliff.'" But Tom saw nothing at the base of the cliff. The ground was bare except for one little bush.

Tom got closer and closer. The VHF signal boomed in his headset. He saw no leopard. He saw no collar. He kept walking. His sons watched from above. They shook their heads. They saw nothing, either.

Until "all of a sudden, there was just an explosion," said Tom, "and this cat came whipping out from behind that bush!" The snow leopard made two bounds. As Tom's sons watched, horrified, from above, the second bound landed six inches from Tom's foot. Green spun to her left, leaped over the next ridge, and was gone.

Tom's sons Kyle (at top) and Keegan (below) try their hand at camel riding and shooting hoops during a break at Bayantooroi.

39

Tom remembers thinking, *So this is what an ibex feels like in its last moments!*

But Green had even more surprises in store.

The satellite data, when it finally came in, was breathtaking. Her home range, calculated over the course of a year, encompassed more than one thousand square kilometers—more than 386 square miles!—an area much larger than anyone ever suspected a snow leopard would ever roam. And she moved around within that range a lot. Green often crossed her entire territory within five days, and Tom estimated she could do it in one or two.

While the satellite recorded data, Tom still looked for Green with his receiver. He still worried about that big collar on the ancient little cat. When they're hunting, snow leopards leap on the prey's back, then lean down and bite the throat to crush the windpipe. When Green hunted, would her big collar get in the way?

One spring day, Tom tracked Green about five miles from camp. The signal was coming from a valley below. Tom stayed on the mountain above her. To his amazement, he spotted her: Lying on a bluff next to a cliff, she seemed as relaxed as a person in a lounge chair on a patio. Lazily, Green got up to stretch. Then she strolled a few steps and began eating . . . because she had just killed a huge male ibex, three times her own weight!

"Obviously the collar wasn't bothering her at all," said Tom. In fact, she had found a use for it. As Tom watched her, "she would eat, lie down, and every time she'd lie down, she'd move her head at an angle and sort of flip her neck," he said. Why? Green was using the telemetry pack on her collar as a pillow!

Green feasted on the ibex for several days and then left. Without seeing her, Tom followed her signal for a year. Then the battery on her collar died.

Toward spring, for some reason, Green's battery came back on. The signal led Tom to her skeleton, lying in a ravine. She had died earlier that winter after a long, wild life—a life that had yielded some of its secrets, to help her kind live on.

FACT

Snow leopards are most active at dawn and dusk.

40

Chapter 8

Rigors of Research

Tom loves nothing more than to be among the world's most spectacular mountains, studying their most elusive big cat.

**O**ur destination: Shat Angiin Am. With Nadia translating, our smiling, twenty-five-year-old guide, Augie, tells Tom this is the best valley for us to search for sign of snow leopards.

Augie should know: his parents and sister pasture their sheep and goats in that valley each spring.

After a half-hour's drive in the van, the landscape changes. It's still rocky brown country, but it's braided with shallow, shimmering streams lined with emerald grass. Tom is pleased with what he sees: above the streams are broken, steep cliffs that ibex love. Snow leopards are sure to follow.

We start our climb at 9:45 a.m., at 5,747 feet. The mountain before us looks like a wall of rock, steep as a cliff. It looks impossible to climb, and nearly is!

Rocks that look like handholds break off in our fingers. Scrambling feet send rocks showering onto the person below. Where to put your foot so it won't slide back down? What handholds will really hold?

It seems to take every muscle in our bodies to pull, push, and haul ourselves up the slope. The top is so distant, we don't dare look too far up ahead—and we sure don't want to look down! Our journey is one of inches, one at a time. There's no other choice.

Steep cliffs make our ascent into the snow leopard's domain difficult.

Kim and Nadia collect scat on an exposed ridge perched high above the valley.

It takes us an hour and a half of agony to reach the top of the ridge. Whew! But to our dismay, it's just an isolated ridge. It leads nowhere, or at least, nowhere a snow leopard or an ibex would want to go.

Tom is stumped. We can't go down the way we came. We'd fall. He scans with binoculars. He finds a small dip between mountains—an area called a saddle—that he thinks we can reach. Maybe from there we can find a way down.

At the saddle, we find a fresh scat. It's filled with red berries, and probably was left by a fox. We collect it anyway. But now what? Where do we go from here, and how?

"Going down the side of this isn't going to be pretty," says Tom. "I was thinking of going over there," he explains, pointing to a distant brown peak, "but it would be hard—hand over hand."

"Straight down?" asks Kim. "Oh, that looks bad." Kim is so fit that she recently completed a 150-mile bike marathon to raise money for charity. Her view of the situation is alarming.

But it's correct.

This long, scree-covered slope seems as steep as the one we came up. But it's worse: going up, you don't have to see the rocks beneath you breaking into a million pieces on their way down—like your body will if you take the wrong step.

But not all the rocks here are loose. Plenty of others are firmly in place. Unfortunately, these look like some giant dropped all his Ginsu knives and they all landed blade-up on a plateau of drying concrete.

We all wish we had more legs. Four would be nice, like an ibex or snow leopard.

We struggle on down. Bruised and bloodied, by 12:45 we're at the valley floor again, back at the starting line.

"I'm not getting the answers I need," says Tom. Where to find better snow leopard territory? We hobble along the sparkling stream, among purple and golden wildflowers. We crisscross the water, hopping from rock to rock. Sometimes Tom extends his walking stick to one of us, and pulls us as we leap across. When we were climbing, mountain breezes kept us cool. But now the sun beats down hard. We tie our polar fleeces and windbreakers around our waists.

At 1:45 p.m. Tom spots a promising cliff. "There! This close range—it looks like very good leopard habitat!" But Augie says another mile away is even better, and easier to get up and down.

So on we go. Is that an ibex on that cliff? Turns out to be a bush. Kim spots the soaring silhouette of a lammergeier ("LAM-er-guy-er"). A huge black and white vulture with a black mask, it has long, narrow wings that make it look like a giant falcon.

At 3:30 we come to the welcome shade of a cliff. Mud from yesterday's rain preserves the delicate paw prints of a Pallas' cat—a secretive, silvery cat with fluffy, dense fur. It weighs only about five pounds.

Here we set down our packs. Should we climb the ridge? We lunch on cheese, bread, and cookies and discuss the options. We're sore. We're sunburned. We're bleeding, bruised, and tired.

Yes, it's decided: Let's go up to have a look.

Across the stream, a herd of twenty-one brown Bactrian camels graze on emerald grass. They look up at us as if we are crazy.

Maybe we are.

FACT

Snow leopards hiss, mew, growl, meow, yowl, and make a puffing sound called prusten as a greeting, but they can't roar.

Domestic camels often graze the valley floors. These camels have nose pegs, to which a rope or reins can be tied when they are led or ridden by people.

Mongolia's Ship of the Desert

It can drink salt water, or go for seven months without drinking at all. Then it can drink up to one quarter of its 1,200-pound weight at a time—twenty-seven gallons. (That would be like you drinking fifty-six cartons of milk!) It can carry 100 pounds of cargo up to thirty miles a day. It can swim, it can wrestle, and it can outrun a horse.

Who is this amazing super-animal? Arabians called it "the gift from God." Marco Polo called it "the ship of the desert." The camel is all this and more.

Camels come with one hump (the Arabian camel or dromedary), two humps (the Bactrian), or none (the four kinds of South American camels: the vicuna, llama, alpaca, and guanaco).

They're all like ninja martial artists. They can kick with all their legs in every direction. The humped camels are great wrestlers, too. (In Turkey, camel wrestling is a popular sport.) Camels can also bite and spit. The spit isn't just drool, either; like cows, camels chew the cud. A gross, green, smelly gob comes shooting out of an angry camel. It pays to be nice to them.

Camels have certainly been nice to humans. For thousands of years these humped hoofers have patiently carried people, their possessions, and their wares over some of the most imposing lands on earth. They're adapted to withstand the worst the desert can offer.

They can shut slitlike nostrils in a sandstorm. They can survive off the fat of their humps for weeks. (A floppy hump means a skinny camel. The hump stands tall again when the camel fattens.)

Because you can cozily sit between its two tall humps,

the Bactrian camel is especially easy to ride. We found out for ourselves when we rode Tom's very own camel outside Bayantooroi. He traded a sewing machine for her nine years ago when she was a baby. He still owns her, but now she grazes with the Great Gobi National Park's fleet of forty-one camels. Far better than jeeps, they provide transportation, milk, wool, and company (and sometimes meat—that's the retirement plan, when the camels get old, over twenty-five or so) as rangers protect the wild animals of the desert.

Tom and his camel.

Chapter 9
Blue Returns

"There are times I ask myself, *What in the world are you doing?*" Tom admitted to us one evening. "*There has got to be an easier animal to study!*"

Tom with Blue, captured the first time.

Sometimes it almost seems the snow leopards are taunting him. Certainly it seemed that way, years ago, with the snow leopard he named Blue. We were eager to hear the story.

After he and his sons had collared Green, Tom told us, he continued to try to track Blue. They hoped they might be able to retrap him, and outfit him with the second satellite collar.

But Blue had other plans.

They heard Blue's radio signal often. About once a week, they would follow him for twenty-four hours straight. Though they couldn't see him, from the pulse of the collar—fast if he was moving, slow if he was lying down—they could tell what Blue was doing. Most leopards are active about one-third of the time (mostly at dawn and dusk) and spend two-thirds of their time resting. But every leopard is different, as are his or her plans every day.

All day, Tom and his sons would follow Blue. All night they would listen from their sleeping bags on a freezing hillside in the whipping wind.

One March day, they tracked Blue about six miles from camp. While Tom followed the radio signal with his antenna, the boys climbed the cliff above him to watch. Tom couldn't see Blue, but the kids could. He was lying next to an ibex kill.

"The kids sat up on a rock and kind of coached me," Tom said. "They'd give me hand signals of how to get down where Blue was." But finally Blue heard the approaching scientist, perhaps one hundred yards away. He fled before Tom ever saw him.

The three rushed back to camp. Now was their chance! They grabbed five snares and drove to the ibex kill. They placed the snares in a circle around it. Surely Blue couldn't resist returning to his meal.

To stay nearby, they decided to spend the night in the jeep. A howling windstorm rocked the vehicle back and forth. Every twenty minutes they had to wake up and turn over the jeep's engine, to make sure the oil wouldn't freeze. They slept only in spurts.

When they woke in the morning, they couldn't wait to check the telemetry.

"There was no signal from Blue at all," said Tom. "He'd left."

They pulled up the snares and went back to camp. Once there, they turned on the radio receiver. The signal was loud and clear. "There was Blue," Tom said, "a couple hundred feet above camp on a ridge line, probably just staring down at us."

About a week later, they discovered that Blue had visited the traps again. But he still wasn't caught. Instead, the snare had accidentally captured an ibex. While the wild goat was stuck in the trap intended for Blue, the leopard had killed and eaten it.

At the end of that winter, the McCarthys tried one last time. They were getting signals from Blue's collar. They knew where he was. They set out a line of traps.

Blue visited the traps, all right, and peed on them.

"It was like a parting shot at us," said Tom: "'You're *not* going to get me!'"

47

FACTS

Scientists found the home territory of a snow leopard ranges from 11 to 23 square miles, in Nepal, to more than 386 square miles, in Mongolia.

Female snow leopards can give birth at age three; males breed at age four.

Chapter 10

Gobi Neighbors

Nadia and Munkho take down the ger.

"U gh!"

"Ow!"

"Ooooooh . . ."

Our groans the next morning go off like an alarm clock. We wake to aching muscles, blistered feet, and searing sunburn from yesterday's hike.

Despite our hard work, the last two days have yielded few samples. "Snow leopards don't give up their secrets easily," says Tom as we breakfast on hot oatmeal in the ger. So it's time to do like the nomads: we're moving camp.

Down comes the ger. Down come our tents. Everything goes back in and on the van. The ger's round *tonoo* caps the softer baggage piled on the roof rack. By 9:15 a.m. the van is loaded. We're off in search of another base camp and another study area.

We're moving farther up the canyon, to an area where Augie says many ibex live. The site is just twelve miles away. Still, on rocky tracks, it's more than an hour's drive.

Just before we reach our new base camp, we stop to chat with our new neighbors. Augie's family's two gers,

Goats wait to be milked. Domestic animals are very valuable to Mongolians and they are cared for well.

housing twelve people including a visiting guest, are pitched just half a mile away.

The soft felt roof of one ger looks like it's got big white tiles on top. Some are round, some are square, and many have beautiful designs. They're not tiles, but a kind of sweet, pressed goat cheese called aarul ("AH-rull") being dried for winter storage. Aarul starts out soft as cottage cheese but bakes hard in the desert sun. How hard? "I hit one once with a rock," Tom tells us, "and it broke the rock."

Luckily, folks out here have teeth strong enough to bite aarul. Maybe it's because of all the milk, cheese, and yogurt they eat.

Every family runs its own dairy. By the front door of the ger, goat milk drips whey from a canvas bag into a bowl. A pot of milk boils on the stove. A big leather bag stores butter beneath a bed. Aarul dries in the sun on every roof.

People milk almost every kind of animal they own: yaks, camels, sheep, goats, and horses. Except (alas) for ice cream, they make every kind of dairy product you can imagine, and some you might not. During our stay we enjoyed thick, sweet yak butter. We tried fizzy, creamy fermented camel's milk. We even sipped vodka made from goat milk!

One day we visit Augie's family while they milk their goats. The herd seems

49

Aarul is made from dried curd. Milk is first heated and then allowed to stand and ferment. Once it has curdled (right-hand bowl), it is strained through a cloth bag so that the clear yellow whey (left-hand bowl) can drain off. Then the strained curd is kneaded and pressed into cakes to be sun-dried on the roof of the ger.

Burneebayor helps
with the milking.

to drift toward the family's compound of gers like a cloud. It takes only six minutes for 170 animals to line up in three columns of about 50 each. One goat faces east and its neighbor faces west. Augie's family helps get them in line. One goat might try to butt in between two others already standing face-to-face. Another might try to escape. But mostly the goats line up by themselves. They've been carefully trained. Just to keep them still, a person ties them together. But they don't seem to mind. Horns almost interlocking, the goats calmly await the milk pail.

Augie's family milks the herd quickly. Only the two-year-old baby is too little to help. Seven-year-old Burneebayor, Augie's older sister's daughter, is already an expert. She has known all of these goats since they were born.

She also knows that some of the family's goats have been eaten by snow leopards, she tells us. We wonder what she thinks of this big predator.

"The snow leopard is a really big animal," Burneebayor tells us as Nadia translates. She hasn't seen one, though the adults have. She's a little afraid of them, she admits. But then Nadia tells her that snow leopards are very rare. Only a tiny handful of areas in just a few

countries have them. Doesn't that make her proud? "Yes!" says Burneebayor. And now she says she hopes one day to see one after all.

Years ago, no one here would have spoken a kind word about the snow leopard. But that was before Tom showed up and, with his colleague Bayara, began to spread the word about these beautiful animals in trouble.

Zandangarar, thirteen years old, is Augie's little sister. She's about to enter seventh grade. She's seen snow leopard photos in school. "It is beautiful!" she tells us through Nadia. "I'm proud to live with such a rare animal." When the leopard eats one of the family's livestock, "we forgive him," she says, "because they don't have a lot of prey."

She thinks about the leopard for a moment. She remembers the beautiful picture from class. The distinctive spots. The long tail. A strong, noble cat who doesn't kill to be mean. A creature, she understands, who belongs here. A fellow citizen of the Gobi, one whom she need not fear. "I will see one someday," she announces.

Zandangarar's purple-blue del is hand-sewn from Chinese silk.

52

Chapter 11

Try, Try Again

Tom stops to take in the breathtaking scenery as we descend to our valley camp.

hree ibex!" calls Nadia.

We've all been scanning the nearby cliffs with binoculars. But Nadia, with her eagle eyes, is the first to spot one of these hardy wild goats—the best sign yet that there should be snow leopards nearby.

Surrounding the ibex are hills so broken it looks like a monster bull ran through a giant's china shop and this is all that's left. The wild goats are standing in a little crater of red rock. Soon Kim picks out six more nearby, all females.

Tom is delighted to see them. "Snow leopard food!"

Several sites near our new base camp look promising. Which, of course, means more steep, rocky climbs.

Our second day at our camp, we hike downstream about two miles. Above us, a rock rolls down a hill. "Who kicked that rock?" Tom asks aloud. "Could be ibex!"

At 9:45 a.m. we begin our climb. Again we grasp for handholds. Again the handholds come off, sickeningly, in our hands. By 10:00 a.m. we're at 8,997 feet. By 10:20 we've reached 9,300.

The air is thinner and we feel it. Gasping for breath, we climb on. Then Kim sees something that makes our hearts pound even harder. In a dusty spot between rocks, faint but unmistakable, is a five-inch-long paw print.

Squinting, we can dimly make out the

Ibex.

FACT

A snow leopard kills a big animal, such as an ibex, only twice a month, and feasts on it for several days. The rest of the month it may snack on smaller animals like pikas, hares, and birds.

imprint of the heel and four oval toe pads. It could be a wolf. But there are no imprints of claws. Only cats can pull their claws in. And only one cat is large enough to leave this print: a snow leopard.

The track is recent. Rain two days ago would have washed an older print away. It was surely left when the ground was still wet. The track is less than two days old.

It's the best proof we've had yet that a snow leopard is living here, now, among us.

A fox is yelling. We can't see it, but we know why it's upset. It's probably a mother or father, distressed we're near its den.

We don't linger. We keep climbing. Our eyes are now fixed on the peak ahead. What will it reveal?

Tom is the first to see.

"Oh, no!"

What could be so awful? We mount the peak to see . . . a blue tent.

What's so bad about a tent? It means that someone is living here, and pasturing animals. "This is good snow leopard habitat," Tom explains, "but snow leopard sign will probably be trampled by livestock."

All we can see ahead are gently rolling hills. Easy walking for us, but no ledges or cliffs or saddles. Nothing a snow leopard would like to mark.

A quick check of the GPS shows we are 5.7 kilometers as the crow flies from camp. If only we could fly! We have

probably walked twice that far already, and it will be at least that far back. All for nothing.

We are tired and sore. "I'm fresh out of ideas," says Tom. Around us stretch miles of rolling hills. It's vast. It's beautiful. But as for snow leopard sign? "Nothing," says Tom. "Absolutely nothing."

On we trek. There's really no choice. We top a mountain covered with loose pink stones. Kim takes a reading on her GPS: we're over eleven thousand feet. Everyone is breathing hard. Tom looks around, frustrated. "It's good snow leopard habitat," he says, "but there are no good marking areas." We'll try again tomorrow.

But within five minutes of starting our hike home, we come upon a pile of scat. It's full of animal hair. Just a few paces later, another. And another. At the edge of a cliff face, we have discovered what may be a common area where the territories of three or four snow leopards overlap!

Some of the scats look recent. Others are old. One contains the leg bone of a pika. In another we find the hoof of an ibex. We find ibex scat as well. And in the larger scats, ibex hair. Both Tom and Augie feel strongly that these scats were left not by wolves, but by snow leopards. The lab will tell us for sure.

Now we've got so many samples, we've run out of plastic bags! We have more

55

The team pauses by a mountain-top ovo, where offerings are made. In keeping with custom, they place pebbles on top while walking clockwise around the ovo.

Our second base camp is set in a beautiful high valley shared by goats.

back at camp. "Given the past five days of collection, who would have guessed we'd have needed to bring more?" Tom asks. We put the scats in plastic gloves. We'll transfer them to bags when we get back to camp.

Another line of scats begins just fifty yards from the last one. Now we're out of gloves! Tom uses his knife to cut pieces from a plastic garbage bag in his pack.

We're tired but happy at the end of our nine-hour hike. Our packs are heavy but our hearts are light. We've collected thirty-four samples today. And we've seen a snow leopard track.

As we slip and slide down the loose rocks of a goat trail toward camp, our ger looks as small as a dime. Our nylon tents are as little as peas. Suddenly we can look at our home from another viewpoint: that of a snow leopard prowling the ridge above. We didn't see a snow leopard. But surely a snow leopard saw us.

Chapter 12
Camera Trap

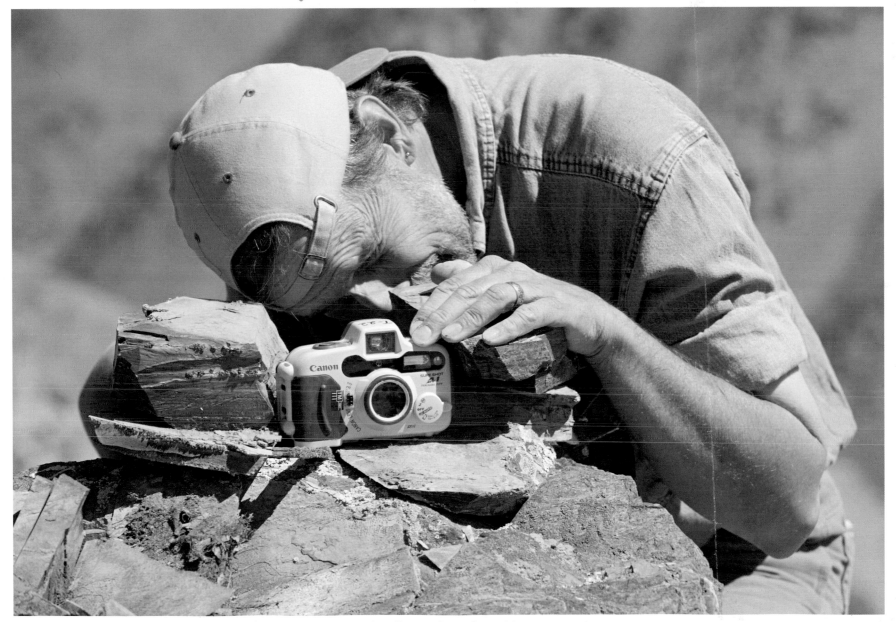

Tom lines up the camera with the spot where the leopard will trip the infrared beam.

There is one more thing Tom needs to do on our expedition: set up the cameras we hope will snap leopard pictures while we're away. Scientists call these specially rigged devices "camera traps" because they capture the animal—on film.

Augie's choice of "mountain boots" amuses the team.

Where to put the cameras? Tom decides to check out one of the ridges in sight of camp. Augie shows up wearing purple plastic bedroom slippers. How hard a hike could it be?

We soon find out.

The slope is so steep that we stop every fifty steps or so. We lean over our walking sticks, gasping for breath, hearts banging. It's hotter today. The sun stings our skin like lemon juice on a cut. Lips crack. Tongues stick. Drops of sweat evaporate before they can roll down our foreheads.

"Is there less oxygen today," jokes Tom, "or more gravity?"

Maybe both, we decide. Except Augie.

In his purple bedroom slippers, he is having no trouble at all.

Eventually we reach the top—1,335 feet above camp, at altitude 9,727 feet.

Disappointment awaits. Little balls of scat everywhere show that livestock graze here often. That's a problem. The camera traps will be rigged to snap a photo of anything big that moves. We don't want twenty-four photos of someone's goats!

"Is there anywhere along that ridge where livestock is *not* grazed?" Tom asks Augie.

Alas, there's not. Two or three families pasture their flocks here. Almost every available area is used, he tells us.

This sharply notched ridge looked a promising place to set up the camera trap

"Let's head down the ridge and see if we find something," says Tom with a sigh.

On we go, scrambling over loose shale, pulling ourselves over knife-blade rocks. We stop along the way to collect scat; there's plenty of it. "If it's snow leopard," says Tom, "he'll be back to re-mark it." The scat is a promising sign.

At last we come to a "pinch point," a sort of passageway from the ridge down the mountain, only as wide as a ger's door. Perfect—or at least, the best spot we've seen so far.

The instruction book for setting up the camera trap begins, "Step one: Select two sturdy trees." Ha! To mount the cameras here in the treeless desert, Tom must find another way. The cameras can't just lie on the bare ground.

Again Tom must improvise. We all scramble to collect rocks of different sizes so that Tom can build small pedestals and shelters for the camera traps.

Selecting the right spot for each camera is important. We need photos of both sides of any leopard who passes. The spot pattern on both sides is needed if the researcher is to identify who's who and get a good count of the leopards in a given area.

But just as important as the angle of the camera is the position of the infrared beam emitter and its receiver. The emitter,

explains Tom, sends a beam of infrared light (outside the spectrum of light that humans or leopards can see) across the top of the leopard's scrape. It will be received by the other device, opposite it. The receiver sends a pulse to the camera to click the shutter when something crosses the beam for three-tenths of a second or longer. (Why three-tenths of a second? So that a fast-flying bird or a piece of blowing grass won't set it off, wasting film.)

After positioning the receiver and emitter, little rock shelters must be built for them. Finally, all the different devices must be connected by cables. We bury the cables carefully under rocks so pikas or goats won't chew them.

But a great many other hazards can befall a camera trap in the wild.

Tom's camera traps have been crunched by bears, licked by leopards, and stolen by people. But those cameras that survive provide important help to scientists. Tom's son Kyle, now a professional wildlife biologist himself, recently used camera traps in Kyrgyzstan and China to identify individual snow leopards and estimate the population size of a certain area. Data from the cameras closely matched the answers he got counting leopards through genetic analysis of collected scats. Using both methods is a good way to check the results of each

for accuracy. And that's mainly what Tom is after with the pair of camera traps we're setting. He wants to have a check against the genetic information.

"Everything's ready," says Tom. "Let's test it. Now, Nadia," he suggests, "crawl this way, onto this scrape. But you don't have to poop on it!"

Everyone laughs.

Obligingly, the young scientist gets down on hands and knees. The flash proves the camera trap is working. The first photo will be of Nadia. But what will the next photo show?

We won't find out for weeks—not till after Tom, Kim, Nic, and I get back to the States.

FACT

Belly fur up to five inches long, as well as a tail nearly as long as the body to wrap around the cat like a muffler, keeps the snow leopard warm at subzero temperatures.

Chapter 13
Yellow's Story

"**P**atience is crucial if you're going to study snow leopards," Tom told us. The rewards of patience can be spectacular. But they aren't always the rewards you expect.

Tom captured Yellow at the entrance to a cave, high in the mountains.

Take, for instance, the story of Yellow.

Yellow was a beautiful young female Tom captured while he and his sons were still trying to recapture Blue. They hadn't really wanted another female. They had hoped to outfit Blue with the other satellite collar, to track a leopard of each sex. But Tom knew that chances to catch a snow leopard are few. He decided to tag and collar Yellow.

And is Tom ever glad he did! The only thing he regrets is that his boys had gone back home to the States by the time he saw Yellow a year later.

"I was tracking Yellow way up on a hillside," he told us, "and I knew she was down below me in a little bowl. I listened to her for a long, long time. Finally she came out of the bushes.

"She came up on a little knoll. I'm watching her and listening to her, and I thought, *How great! I've finally seen one of my cats!—which is so rare.*"

Yellow kept looking back down at the place where she had first emerged from the bushes. Why?

Tom had an idea. Bet you do, too. "Sure enough, a couple minutes later, out of the brush come these three little roly-poly snow leopards, tripping all over each other, bounding along, going up for Mom. And they'd just got up to their mother and they're playing with her and she's just kind of sitting there looking around. And I was behind a rock, at least a hundred and fifty yards from her.

"I hadn't budged," Tom remembers. "And all of a sudden she just turned and looked up at me, and looked square into my binoculars. She looked me right in the eye. And you could just see the look on her face. It was like, You're *not* supposed to be here!"

Immediately the mother turned and raced to her cubs. Urgently she nudged them with her nose, then padded up a hillside with the cubs behind. Where the slope got steeper, she went back to help. She picked up one cub in her mouth and dropped it out of Tom's sight. She meowed at the others to hurry on.

Tom tracked Yellow's signal for the rest of the day. Then the family holed up.

"I spent the rest of the summer trying to get a look at those cubs," said Tom. "Yellow would *never* let me close enough to see those cubs again. And I never saw her again, either. She was such a good mother."

It is the only time so far that he's seen snow leopard cubs in the wild.

Chapter 14

Knitting It All Together

62

Gangur's yaks gallop down from the hills for milking.

It starts with a deep, far-off rumble, like thunder. But there are no rain clouds in the sky. Dust rises like smoke in the distance. We hear deep, meaningful grunting, sounds a mountain might speak. And then, over the rise, we see them.

Gangur's yaks are coming home.

Standing by our new friend's ger, we watch in awe. The shaggy herd gallops toward us. The yaks' thick coats hang down to their ankles. As they run, their fur streams like flowing robes. With their long, curving horns and shaggy bellies and tails, these huge animals look prehistoric—and in fact, they are. Long before there were people to call them oxen, sure-footed yaks, the males weighing two tons, roamed Asia's high, snowy steppes. Wild yaks still do.

Gangur's seventy yaks are just a few of his thousand animals. Gangur is the seventy-eight-year-old father of a family of ten. Besides his wife, kids, and yaks, he also has forty horses, ten camels, and hundreds of goats and sheep. Three of his adult children and three of his many grandchildren live with him and his wife. Their grand compound includes three spacious, beautiful gers.

We're visiting them with Bayara, who has just joined the expedition. Together we're going from one ger to another, talking with families who are part of Snow Leopard Enterprises—the centerpiece of the Snow Leopard Trust's conservation plan.

Gangur sips fermented yak milk from a silver bowl.

The ceremonial dish called buuz is made by wrapping ground mutton in disks of hand-rolled dough to make little "parcels," which are steamed.

64

Mongolians are generous hosts. At each home we visit, we're offered huge platters of aarul. We drink gallons of milk tea. One hostess offers to slaughter a goat for us. (We politely decline, so she makes us delicious dumplings called buuz ["boze"] instead.) We're even invited to a wedding!

But most important of all, visiting with families like Gangur's gives us a taste of how people's feelings about snow leopards have changed—and how that changes the leopard's future.

"It's amazing," Gangur says, with Bayara translating. "You can't really see the snow leopard. That's why people call it a ghost." Forty years ago, searching for a lost goat, Gangur was following the tracks of a snow leopard and a fox. At the end of the tracks, he found the fox, but not the snow leopard.

If he had, he would have shot it. In those days, the Soviets paid a bounty for every snow leopard killed, Gangur explained. People hated snow leopards. Some thought they sucked blood like vampires and got drunk on blood.

All that is changing. "Snow leopards are getting rare," Gangur said. "I don't like to see anyone shoot wildlife in my area. I feel sorry for the animals."

But besides feeling sympathy, Gangur also knows how he and his fellow herders can help—and that they'll be nicely rewarded if they do.

In exchange for the promise not to hunt snow leopards or their natural prey, herder families can join Snow Leopard Enterprises, as did Gangur's family seven years ago. The program is extremely popular. Participants learn new skills, earn extra income, and gain new confidence.

And it all started with a sweater.

When Bayara first started talking with local herders, they were angry. Acting as Tom's translator, she would accompany him on visits with local people and ask them how they felt about snow leopards. The answers were always the same.

"Snow leopards ate my livestock!" they would tell her. "Why can't we kill them?"

That was in 1996. Laws had only recently been passed to protect the endangered cats. But laws are no good unless people obey them.

Tom and Bayara tried to explain. They told the people the cats were endangered. They told them why they attacked livestock: the leopards didn't have any choice. "And then we got the idea," Bayara told us, "that there could be some kind of program that local people could be involved in to help conserve the snow leopards. But how could we involve them? How could we encourage them to help the animals?"

During one of their discussions, Bayara was knitting a sweater for Tom out of beautiful, soft camel wool yarn. She realized she might have the solution in her hands. "Maybe this is something we can use!" she cried.

From her talks with the herders, Bayara knew

Camel wool is hand-spun into yarn, which will then be knitted to make scarves to sell through Snow Leopard Enterprises.

65

that they sometimes sold their animals' wool to local traders to earn cash for things items like cloth, pots, sugar, and flour. But the herders didn't get much money. Why not teach them to make products from the wool and help them sell the wares for more money in America? But only families who promised not to kill leopards could join. If a leopard was killed in their area, they couldn't take part in the program.

With British colleague Priscilla Allen, Tom and Bayara started Snow Leopard Enterprises in 1998, and began working with fifty families. It took time for the herders to perfect their products. At first the scarves were too scratchy. The socks were too small for Americans. "We could have said, 'Oh, we can't buy this,'" Bayara recalls. "But we bought everything they made—to create trust."

Gradually, the herders improved their skills. The products are now first-class. Americans love camel-wool socks and mittens, yak-wool scarves and yarn. And instead of a Hacky sack, you can buy a Yaky-sack: it's made from yak-wool felt and filled with Gobi stones!

The herders' work is sold in zoos, through Snow Leopard Trust's website, and in yarn shops. Four hundred families now participate in seven Mongolian provinces. The Snow Leopard Trust has expanded its program to other countries, too.

One woman we visit tells us she uses the extra income to buy books for her children. At another ger, a father explains that through Snow Leopard Enterprises, his daughter not only sells felt, but now has learned how to make beautiful felt slippers for her own kids. Another family tells us they hope to use the money they make from Snow Leopard Enterprises to send their daughter to medical school.

And whom can the families thank for the extra income and newfound skills? Their former enemy, the snow leopard.

"We have to protect snow leopards," fifty-one-year-old Surenjav tells us on the day we visit her ger. She and her daughter make scarves. "Snow leopards are rare," Surenjav explains. "If they were to disappear, things would change." In study after study, scientists have proven that Surenjav is right: removing top predators upsets entire ecosystems. It even changes the numbers and kinds of microorganisms in the *soil!* Without predators such as snow leopards, prey animals can overpopulate and spread diseases, and wild animals can transmit sickness to livestock. "Everything," Surenjav says, "is connected."

And that's the best thing about the program, Bayara says: it teaches people why their own lives are better with snow leopards around.

Without that understanding, conservation can't succeed. "The people who live in this area, they have to be the owner of this land, the owner of this mountain, the owner of this wildlife," Bayara says. "This is their conservation program. Not ours. It is their land, their snow leopard. But we can help!"

One day, Gangur told us, he was passing a sharp cliff. He caught a rare sight: A snow leopard was looking directly into his eyes. "His face was calm," he said, "and not angry. It is a very majestic animal. Not scared of anything—just peaceful and calm."

FACT

Snow leopards usually give birth to two to three cubs in a litter, but litters of up to seven cubs have been born in zoos.

Chapter 15
How to Save a Ghost

Toward the end of our fieldwork together, Tom looked back to see all of us climbing behind him. He knew exactly what we were thinking: *Please, snow leopard, step out! Let us see you—just a glimpse!*

Tom and Nadia use the back of the van as a mini lab to sort scat samples for shipping back to the United States.

He was right. He knew, because he used to think this all the time. "The first few years, I was always looking. I might see a leopard! What if a snow leopard walked around that rock right now? Or if I saw one lying on a cave doorstep?"

That sure would be terrific. But now Tom knows he might well go another nine years without seeing a leopard again. And that's OK with him.

His work offers plenty of excitement. "It's thrilling to be out in this habitat," he says. "It's thrilling to be up in the highest peaks of the world and learn about the different cultures. And think of how many leopards walked down that hillside that you walked today. You saw—what? Twenty-five scats today? From multiple leopards! You're walking in the track of that cat even though you don't see it. That's pretty special. That's something very, very few people ever get to do."

In the end, though, says Tom, the work is not just about excitement. "It all comes down to what you can do for this incredible animal," Tom says. "If you can just add a little bit to the likelihood of their long-term survival, then you've done something important."

And that we have done.

We've collected seventy-eight scat samples that will help Tom determine how many leopards live in the valley we explored. We have visited and interviewed dozens of herding families. We have encouraged local people to appreciate the treasure in their own backyards.

"Even sitting here in this field camp is helping snow leopards," Tom told us. "Because the people over there in that ger are saying, 'Look at these people who came halfway around the world just to look for the tracks of this animal—an animal which five years ago we despised and now we tolerate. And maybe now we ought to think about liking it! Everyone else seems to.' Just the fact that we're here tells people this is something special up here in their mountains."

But what about the answers to the questions Tom is asking? What happened to the camera traps? Which of the seventy-eight scats we collected were leopards' and which were not? How many leopards live in the valleys we sampled?

Right before we left our second base camp with Bayara, Augie retrieved the camera traps and emitters. We checked the first camera to see how many pictures it had snapped. It showed only one, and we knew it was Nadia!

Had nobody crossed that beam? Not even a sheep or a pika? We looked at the second camera. Though the first camera had malfunctioned, the second had taken a full roll. Back in Ulaanbaatar, Bayara got the film developed.

Nadia e-mailed us with the results: after the first test shot of her crawling on hands and knees, the camera had taken twenty-three photos . . . of a herder's goats.

And as for the other data? As we take this book to press, we still don't know. Which scats were leopards' and which were not won't be answered until the dogs have analyzed the samples. Not until winter will we learn from the genetics lab about how many of the scats belonged to leopards.

Even then, we won't have enough information yet to know if the snow leopard population is growing or shrinking, or whether Snow Leopard Enterprises is really helping leopards in this area after all. To get those answers, we'll have to keep coming back, again and again.

Sound frustrating? It can be! But Tom, Kim, Nadia, and Bayara, as well as most other people working to conserve endangered animals, look at it another way.

Protecting an animal is like loving someone. It's not something you do and then finish. It's a long-term promise, honored over and over, one step at a time. Sort of like climbing those ridges to find where the next ridge leads, and the next one.

"We can't know everything right away," Nadia told as we were leaving Mongolia. "It's step by step. In a movie or on TV, it seems they know everything in an hour. But it really takes a long time."

And perhaps it's better that way, because the commitment, and the adventure, continue.

Tom's Advice to Young Conservationists

Being a research biologist like Tom isn't easy. Yet Tom insists, "If you have a dream to do science, don't let anybody tell you that you can't do it."

But climbing cliffs and collecting poop aren't the only ways to save a cat. "There's all different ways to be involved," says Tom. "You don't have to be a field biologist like me."

Consider all the ways in which people help save snow leopards: Some, like Bayara, interview and work with local people. Some make and sell products. Others work in laboratories or pore over GPS coordinates. Some work as veterinarians, some as fundraisers, others as teachers, and more.

"You might be working at the government level, helping to develop wildlife management plans," says Tom. "You could be working to build stronger treaties and international agreements."

Politics, economics, biology, teaching, sociology: whatever your passion, you can use it to help snow leopards survive.

70

FACT

Snow leopard cubs stay with Mom for eighteen to twenty-two months.

The Snow Leopard Trust

Founded in 1981 by the late Helen Freeman, a former teacher, the Snow Leopard Trust is the world's oldest and largest organization devoted entirely to saving snow leopards. Trust representatives may be visiting your area. They would be happy to arrange a talk at your school. Check out the trust's wish list—from sleeping bags to binoculars—and see if you have something to donate. Hold a fundraiser and adopt a snow leopard. You'll receive a stuffed-toy snow leopard for your efforts and will know your money is helping a real snow leopard in the wild. Buy beautiful hand-knit scarves, mittens, socks, and other items created by families like Gangur's. Visit the trust's website at www.snowleopardtrust.org to learn how you, your family, your school, or your class can help.

Acknowledgments

Let's Speak Mongolian

Under Communist rule, the original Mongol script introduced by Genghis Khan was replaced by a modified alphabet much like Russia's. Unfortunately, it doesn't translate to how Mongolian words really sound. To make things easier, we spell the words below the way they would be pronounced if they were written in English—or as close as we can come.

How are you? **Sehn bahn OH?**
I'm fine. Sehn.
Are your sheep fattening up nicely?
   Mal SUE-reg tar gan tav TIE oh?
Yes. Teem.
Hey, I'm just outside your ger! (This actually translates to "Hold the dog!")
   Nokho KHOR—ee-oh!

Camel **TIM-ay**
Snow leopard **EAR-biss**
Yak **SAR-lag**
I want to ride a camel.
   Bee TIM-ay yav-akh gesen yum.
I like snow leopards. **Bee EAR-biss derr ty.**
Thank you. **By ar LAH.**
Goodbye. **By ar TAI.**

For all they taught us, we thank our scientific colleagues as well as the wonderful Mongolian families we met during our visit.

In addition, for their help in organizing our expedition, assisting with photos, and researching, fact checking, and editing the manuscript, we thank Joan Ahern; Catherine Cluett; Dr. Lisa Dabek; Cindy Dickenson; Elizabeth Marshall Thomas; Dr. Gary Galbreath; our great editor, Kate O'Sullivan; the Woodland Park, Brookfield, and John Ball zoos (where Nic's photos of snow leopards and ibex were taken), and the staff of the Snow Leopard Trust.

A Note from the Author

For an author, every book presents new challenges. For me, sometimes it's avoiding being eaten by my study subjects—like when I wrote about man-eating tigers in India. Sometimes, it's swimming for hours in swift current—like when I was researching my book on pink dolphins. For this book, my big problem was trying not to fall off the mountain.

Hiking in the woods with our border collie the spring before our summer expedition, I tripped over a fallen tree and sprained my ankle so badly that I needed crutches for three weeks. With the help of personal trainers, I worked hard for months to get back in shape for the strenuous climb in the Altai Mountains. Then, the Tuesday before our flight to Mongolia, I fell in a chipmunk hole by our barn and twisted my ankle again.

Once we reached snow leopard territory, I kept falling down. My friends would look behind them and find me sprawled on the ground. With each new fall, I grew increasingly unstable on slopes slippery with rocky scree. Nic picked me up again and again. He was highly motivated to save me: he had his hands full taking the photos and sure didn't want to have to write this book, too! Trying to help, Kim urged, "Be one with the rock." But that was just what I feared: that with a single slip on the wrong slope, I would suddenly be reduced to splatter on stone. I surely would have been were it not for Nic's strength and patience, and the kindness and care of our colleagues on this trip, always willing to extend a hand.

Another challenge was the cuisine. I am a vegetarian. The Mongolian diet is based almost exclusively on meat and milk. Outside the cities, that's almost all there is to eat. Eating a salad, for instance, is an almost unimaginably alien idea. In Mongolian culture, only animals eat leaves. Happily, our talented and hard-working cook, Enke, prepared lovely meatless meals for me at camp. At a dinner party at Nadia's parents' house, her mom made me special vegetarian buuz. But problems arose when we visited people's gers. Almost everywhere we stopped, we were offered meat—and sometimes our hosts offered to kill an animal in our honor! How could I refuse their hospitality?

Vegetarianism makes no sense in a culture in which a plant-based diet is simply not an option. I'm not completely sure how our Mongolian colleagues explained to our hosts why I don't eat meat. Possibly our hosts imagined I had some terrible disease. But even so, thanks to the extraordinary generosity of the strangers who make hospitality a way of life in the desert, no one ever acted insulted when I couldn't eat their meat. They gave me tea, aarul, and bread instead. I always felt welcome in every ger, and treated like an honored, if perhaps eccentric, guest.

A Note from the Photographer

An expedition like this is a mixture of exhilaration and exhaustion. Within a few days, you go from the comfort of home to being bounced around in the back of a vehicle, crossing hundreds of miles of the Gobi Desert. The temperature is 110 degrees Fahrenheit, your biological clock is adrift by twelve time zones, and everything has changed: the language, the food, and the customs. And you really are not sure where you are, where you're going, or exactly what you will find if you get there.

It would be easy to feel overwhelmed and completely exhausted at such times. But I know I can't. I have less than three weeks to illustrate an entire book with photos, which means I have to be alert and able to take a new and exciting picture every two or three hours of every single day.

I deal with this as best I can by making sure that I am as fit and healthy as possible beforehand. I work out for hours each week at the gym and on my road bike. But there are still worrying thoughts that linger at the back of my mind. My three main concerns were first, having a vehicle break down in the Gobi, since you could die of thirst long before another vehicle came by (here I have to thank my wife for the very sensible suggestion that I carry a satellite phone); second, falling ill without medical help, which luckily didn't turn out to be a problem apart from my being flattened by heatstroke for a day or so in the Gobi; and third, flying on types of planes that I had never heard of before, except in accident reports. Sy and I were a bit apprehensive when our pilot on the homeward leg in Mongolia said our plane was not safe unless it flew half empty of passengers. I just held my breath till we landed.

The main challenge for photography was dust—which is everywhere in the Gobi. I had to seal all my equipment in layers of plastic bags and carefully clean it after every use. The other issue was not having access to power, so I took a mountain of batteries to last about three weeks.

There were many wonderful highlights to the trip. The barren Altai Mountains were unlike any place I had been to before. But best of all, I think, was the hospitality of the nomadic herders. They were always so welcoming and very patient with us when we did not understand their customs. And best of all, for me, they loved to have their photographs taken.

Of course I never expected to photograph a snow leopard in the wild. Some people have asked if I was disappointed not even to see a wild snow leopard. But in many ways I am happy not to see one. I love that some things in nature will always remain mysterious and unseen. Just knowing that they are out there is pleasure enough.

To Learn More:

Learn what books the author read to research this book. Read excerpts from the author's field diary. Try a recipe for Mongolian dumplings. For all this and more, visit www.authorwire.com and click on the image of this book.

To see more photos from Mongolia and around the world and to learn more about photographer Nic Bishop, visit www.nicbishop.com.

72

Index

Page references to illustrations and sidebars are in **bold** typeface.

73

74